BADGERS

First published in Great Britain in 1998 by
Colin Baxter Photography Ltd.,
Grantown-on-Spey,
Moray PH26 3NA
Scotland

Text © John Darbyshire 1998
Photographs © Laurie Campbell 1998
All rights reserved

A CIP Catalogue record for this book is available from the British Library

ISBN 1-900455-58-7

Printed in Hong Kong

BADGERS

John Darbyshire & Laurie Campbell

Colin Baxter Photography, Grantown-on-Spey, Scotland

Contents

Introduction

Many people may never see a wild badger; many others will only see it as a dead creature lying by the side of the road. But if you take some time to find a sett, and creep into the woods as evening approaches, then with a little luck you will catch a glimpse of Britain's largest surviving carnivore. The sight of that sensitive nose emerging to carefully test the air, followed by the striped head, captivates watchers again and again. It is a sight that remains with people all their lives and is often the starting point of a lifetime's involvement for thousands of people who have fallen under its spell. So it was with me, caught in the magic of the woods in the gloaming, a latent hunter stalking through the trees in search of the denizen of the woods.

My first encounter with a badger was in the summer of 1977 when cycling up Kirkstone Pass in the Lake District. It was after 11pm and quite dark, when a shadowy figure on the grass verge caught my eye. Startled by my silent approach, a badger hurtled out onto the road straight into the path of my bicycle. I hit the beast, toppled from my bike and landed right on top of the animal. He let out a fierce growl and made off, leaving me prostrate on the road, bewildered but unharmed. The next morning I pulled a badger hair from the brake lever and since then I have always recognised their coarse, white hair with a black band near the tip. It was a decade before I came so close again, first caring for an injured animal that had been hit by a car, then another caught in a snare, and then an orphaned cub. Now badger queries and questions come to me every day, ranging from people who want to watch and help in their conservation, to others who find them causing problems in their gardens or because their setts are in the line of a new road or opencast mine.

Since that early encounter I have watched badgers countless times, often nightly, and sometimes all through the night, following them from their sett and out into the open countryside on their wanderings.

These badger cubs will be fully grown by the time they are one year old.

General Characteristics

This book concentrates on the Eurasian badger (*Meles meles*), the animal familiar to the UK. They are carnivores by classification yet are omnivores by habit, eating both animal and plant material. This is reflected in their back teeth which are greatly modified for crushing and grinding. Compare this for a moment with the dentition of a fox whose premolars and molars are markedly chisel-shaped for cutting flesh and bone. Badgers evolved from animals similar to today's pine marten, around 60 million years ago, and the first badger-like fossils appeared 4 million years ago in the temperate forests of Asia. It is from here that they spread to Europe. They weigh on average around 22 lbs (10 kgs) with a length of around 3.3 ft (1 m). The weights vary between the sexes with males usually being just over 2 lbs (1 kg) heavier than the females, weights also vary considerably throughout the year. They are heaviest toward the end of autumn when they have the most fat reserves, and correspondingly lightest in late spring when they have used up all their reserves, and food is most difficult to find. They are extraordinary diggers. Their strong front claws, backed up by powerful shoulder muscles, help them dig their sometimes huge setts, and assist in digging for food such as wasps' nests and grubs. They have been known to move a boulder weighing 55 lbs (25 kgs) to get at food underneath it!

Badgers don't usually live longer than ten years in the wild; captive animals have lived for as long as 19 years, but this is exceptional. It is possible to tell something of a badger's age from looking at tooth wear. A badger's diet includes a large amount of earthworms and during feeding the earth causes the white enamel of their teeth to wear down from an early age. I have seen the yellow dentine showing through the enamel in animals that are not yet fully grown. In old animals the teeth can be practically worn away and one wonders how they have managed to survive.

The most striking physical feature of the badger is its head stripe. Not only is it

Unlike a human's, a badger's world relies on scents.

With the advancing darkness the badger's body all but
disappears, leaving only its striped head visible.

usually the first thing to be seen when looking for a badger in the woods, but it is often the only visible part of the animal as it moves through the darkness. Its primary function would appear to be that of a warning to potential aggressors. Just as a wasp instils caution despite its diminutive size, so a badger's warning is backed up by a very powerful bite. However, occasionally a badger will cover its stripes with its paws or run away with its head held low. These actions seem to be the reverse of an aggressive stance and appear to indicate that at times discretion is the better part of valour.

With regard to badger aggression, I am often asked if badgers attack pets in the garden, or even people. They do sometimes kill pet rabbits or guinea pigs, taking them from cages that are not badger-proof. As to attacking people, for years I confidently stated that this was not the case, until two incidents in 1997 led me to reconsider. The first was a letter from a hill-walker and photographer. He

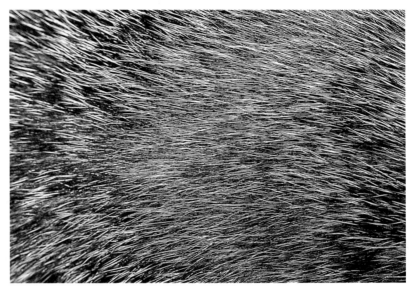

Banded hairs give the badger its overall grey colour.

had been over three thousand feet up a Scottish mountain, busily engaged in taking a picture, when what he thought was his dog began to pull and worry at his trouser leg. He shook his leg to get rid of the dog, but it would neither stop nor let go. Irritated, he looked down and was shocked to see not his dog, but a badger. At this point his little dog rushed the badger and a scuffle ensued, during which the dog was bitten on its belly. Man and dog began to run down the mountain, pursued by the badger. After a short chase the badger stopped, fluffed itself up to its greatest size and let out a low growl. The baffled walker then realised that to have any chance of being believed he had to get a picture of the beast, which he did. The picture clearly shows an angry badger and a rocky mountain top. In the shop at the foot of the mountain the story was related. The shopkeeper wasn't in the least bit surprised and added that a local badger had recently killed one of the gamekeeper's dogs.

On another occasion, I was walking through the woods at about 11pm when I was rushed by a badger. It stopped about three feet away, fluffed up to its greatest size and uttered a deep growling noise. I had no alternative but to stand there and hope, which seemed to pay off, as after a few seconds, it turned and went off noisily through the wood.

Digging is dirty work.

Badgers have an extraordinary sense of smell and indeed much of their lifestyle is governed by the information they receive through their nose. This includes, searching for food, recognising danger, identifying other members of their group or intruders from other areas, and finding their way around their territory. Their snout is relatively large and flexible, so that they are able to move it out of the way when foraging for food. This enables them to use their teeth to tear up bulbs or catch grubs, while at the same time avoiding any damage to their sensitive nose. When watching badgers emerge from their sett or when they spend prolonged periods out in the fields you may notice that they repeatedly push their noses in the air to search for the slightest scent. Inexperienced watchers may misinterpret this and think they are being looked at, but it is more likely they are being smelled.

Badger cubs must learn to find food quickly in readiness for their first winter.

The substantial front claws of a badger are perfect for digging; backed up by powerful shoulder muscles, they are capable of excavating tons of soil. Scratches can be found where they have scrambled over logs and rocks. Elder and soft-barked trees are favourite scratching posts.

Lifestyle and Habitat

The Eurasian badger is just one of a number of animals which share a common ancestry. The others include pine martens, which have taken to the tree tops; otters, which took to the rivers and sea shore; polecats, now restricted to localised areas; stoats, which turn to ermine in the colder areas of the land; and, last but not least, weasels, the smallest and most ferocious of them all, which give the rest their general family name, the weasels.

In the UK, badgers live in mountains, woodlands, towns, sea cliffs and roadsides, inhabiting landscapes from the northern tip of Scotland to the south coast of England. A quarter of the UK's population is to be found in the south-west of England, and a few badgers are found on some of the islands, including Arran, where they were introduced in the eighteenth century for sport. The UK population is witnessing a recovery due to the increasing enlightenment of large sporting estates and their gamekeepers, coupled with the increasing activities of badger groups around the country who, together, have contributed to changes in legislation which have led to further protection. *The Badgers Act 1992* gave legal protection to badgers and their setts and it is now an offence to disturb or ill-treat them. Despite all this positive work, however, there are still large areas of the country where there are no badgers, even though the habitat is ideal. In some woodlands there are setts that have not been occupied for years because of past and present persecution.

The Eurasian badger is predominantly a woodland animal, and if the country was covered with dense forests, as it was thousands of years ago, badgers would be quite happy. These primeval forests have all but disappeared and in their place are small woodlands, fields, hedgerows, villages and cities. The badger has successfully adapted to and colonised all these diverse habitats yet still remains absent from around 60% of lowland Britain. Today its increasing presence in our countryside

Broadleaved woodland is the preferred habitat for badgers.

17

*As population levels increase, badgers move out of woodlands and into less
favoured areas such as open fields, hedgerows and the urban fringe.*

serves as a litmus test of the state of the environment and our attitude to it.

Badgers eat a wide variety of food, though earthworms make up about half of their intake. Other foods include insects and their grubs, fruits and berries, small mammals which they can dig up and, in the autumn, grain from the fields. Their catholic diet and ability to cause damage when finding food, sometimes brings them into conflict with farmers, who can find grain fields damaged, or turf that has been grown for lawns dug up in the search for grubs. When badgers cause serious damage, there is provision within the legislation to mitigate the worst effects and find a solution. A healthy population of any creature at the top of its food chain indicates that the food throughout the chain is plentiful and relatively unaffected by pollution, pesticides and disease. As otters are to rivers, badgers are to woodlands – an indicator of the health of the ecosystem of which they are a part.

Sett entrance and large spoil heap.

Badgers prefer peaceful woodlands and hedgerows for the location of their setts. Often impressive structures, the setts can have a network of as much as half a mile (1 km) of twisting and turning underground tunnels. The spoil heaps at the entrances can be truly enormous, containing literally tonnes of soil and old bedding, dragged out decade after decade and dumped unceremoniously down the hillside.

Badgers spend more than half their lives underground. Much of that time they are curled up asleep in small chambers about the size of a bean bag. Although they usually sleep alone, when it is cold they will curl up with one or two other badgers, squeezed into a small space to conserve heat. The sett is cleverly designed, often dug into a hillside which reduces digging effort, and into strata that will not collapse but are not too difficult to dig. The chambers are most often situated above the entrance. This allows cold air to sit in the U-bend while the rising warmer air helps the chamber retain heat. The tunnels and chambers are seldom more than 6.5 ft (2 m) underground and often not far from the surface. Occasionally the roof of a chamber collapses, and these resulting holes may then be used as new entrances with very steep descents. Badgers habitually collect bedding

A badger drags bedding backwards into the sett.

of dry grasses and leaves to make a nest to sleep on, and it is not uncommon to find one of these bundles discarded when a badger was disturbed whilst gathering it.

Close inspection of these bundles often reveals a tell-tale badger hair. There is also circumstantial evidence that they collect green bedding material. It is assumed that the badgers have learned that as this fresh material decays it gives off heat, warming the chamber further. In amongst all this bedding material, fur and heat, live the much maligned parasites: lice, fleas, ticks and mites. Although high external parasite loads will not directly kill a badger, intestinal parasites can.

Badgers are well adapted to their underground way of life. They have stiff hairs on the snout to help them feel their way in dark passages. Their eyesight, though not good, is best adapted to half-light conditions, and this suits them well in the gloomy woods. For their size, they are immensely strong with long front claws, ideally built for digging. Indeed the word 'badger' comes from the French word *becheur,* for digger. It is from these labyrinthine structures that the badgers emerge at dusk to find food, patrol their territory and, when the time is right, find a mate.

Bedding material is discarded after use and can be found in the spoil heap.

The Badger's Year

Female badgers start to give birth to cubs from January, and by the end of March most births have taken place. Being born early in the year is important for a badger, as the young animals need plenty of time to eat, grow and put on fat, before the rigours of their first winter. In Britain the majority of cubs are born in mid February, earlier in the south and later in the north.

Mid February is also a peak mating time, as females come into oestrus soon after the birth of their cubs. Badgers can, however, mate at any time of the year and still bear their cubs in the early spring.

This story of reproduction is intriguing and complex. It begins with the dominant male (boar) and female (sow) of a clan of badgers that may number between 5 and 12 animals. As in many species, the dominant animals instinctively need to ensure that their genes are passed on to the next generation. The dominant male's strategy is quite straightforward and is based on intimidation and superior strength. He uses these tactics at peak breeding times to brow-beat the other males into submission so that he has the best chance of mating. It is a common sight when watching badgers early in the year to see bite marks and wounds above the tail where young badgers have been attacked and injured by older, more experienced ones. This can sometimes lead to a number of subordinate males occupying outlying setts while waiting for their chance to breed. From these setts they can also make forays into adjoining territories with the chance of an opportunistic mating.

It is likely that the dominant female uses a similar tactic of aggression to a subordinate sow, most probably when cubs are born, and infanticide is not unknown. The sows often mate both with the dominant male and with other males from adjacent territories when they are in breeding condition. As a result of these matings each female's uterus can hold a number of eggs, fertilised by different males, at

After the birth of cubs, the sow must find plenty of food.

different times of the year. However the litters of cubs will all be born during the early spring. This is achieved by delayed implantation: the fertilised eggs do not implant in the uterine wall but remain in suspension, barely developing, all through the spring, summer and autumn. By mid December the time for these clusters of cells (blastocysts) to implant in the uterine wall draws near, and by the end of the month gestation will have begun.

Six or seven weeks after implantation the cubs are born. A litter can number as many as five cubs, but two or three is more usual. The cubs are about 4.7 in (120 mm) long at birth, with a sparse covering of hair which often shows the characteristic eye stripe, or will do so within a few days of birth. The cubs do not open their eyes until they are around five weeks old, and will not emerge from the sett until April or May.

During the breeding season and while the birth of cubs is underway, the dominant male is very active, marking the boundary of a territory, which can vary in size from as small as 37 acres (15 ha) in the high density areas of the south, to upwards of 250 acres (101 ha) or more where both badgers and food are harder to come by, in more mountainous regions for example. He marks the area using dung pits, secretions from his subcaudal gland (located under the base of his tail), and, more so in summer and autumn, his urine. The reasons for this vigilance are thought to be, firstly to protect the food supply, and secondly to keep females from mating with marauding male intruders.

In early spring the females are busy raising and feeding the cubs. When the cubs are underground the female is especially vigilant and she often uses a specially prepared chamber, separate from the rest of the sett, with its own entrance. Male badgers are not welcome and are driven away, but there is growing evidence that subordinate females may take an active role in helping the mother by baby-sitting when the mother is out foraging. It is at this time that badgers are most vulnerable, so any potential threats, such as a passing fox, are soon driven away.

Around eight weeks after birth, during late April and early May, badger cubs

Most cubs emerge in April or May. Naturally wary at first, they soon become boisterous and playful, following their mother on foraging trips into nearby fields.

During the late summer when food is plentiful, badgers eat and store fat in readiness for the rigours of winter. Winter is a time of high mortality, especially for the old and young.

take their first tentative steps out into the world, and are soon playing all kinds of games, and rough and tumble. At this age they have relatively little awareness of the dangers from dogs and man, so the mother and the cubs often appear to move as one animal, as they begin to explore the world. At the sett I visit regularly I once watched a cub playing with a discarded tin. It picked up the tin and carried it about 65 ft (20 m) up the slope. Upon dropping it, it chased the tin back down the slope, tumbling head over heels as it did so. The cub repeated this game time and time again.

As the weeks pass the cubs become more boisterous. They can be seen playing games similar to tag, or 'king of the castle' on an old tree stump, or grabbing an adult's tail to be hauled about. Soon the cubs accompany their mother on foraging trips into the surrounding fields, and at this time the cubs never take their noses from under their mother's, as they learn how to find food.

As mid summer approaches food becomes more abundant and the badgers have less trouble finding it. Life is a little easier and the animals begin to put on weight. As summer advances, there is a superabundance of caterpillars on the cabbages in the fields and the badgers become the farmer's friend by eating enormous quantities of them. Trees and shrubs begin to fruit, and the badgers feed on blaeberry and raspberry. Badgers eat many different kinds of berries and this is reflected in the plants that can be seen in the vicinity of the sett, or at areas where there are latrines. It is not uncommon to see elder, rowan, blackberry, and raspberry that have been planted by the badgers after the seeds have been through their gut. Also associated with latrine sites are stinging nettles, which grow in the nitrate-rich soil.

At summer's end and through the autumn putting on fat is a priority and the badgers are busy eating as much as they can in readiness for the long lean months ahead. As November moves into December badgers are at their most inactive and stay underground for extended periods of time. Whilst they do not hibernate they can go into a deep sleep called a torpor which can last for days at a time. In January badgers begin to get more active as the breeding season approaches, and the female in particular begins to prepare the sett for the birth of cubs.

Although carnivores, badgers feed on a wide variety of plant material. They are especially partial to autumn fruits.

On damp nights worms come to the surface of the earth and are easily caught.
Badgers can, however, root for prey with their nose, raking away the ground with
their powerful claws in search of other grubs, and bulbs of bluebell and pignut.

Badgers and Conservation

Without a doubt, there has been an association between badgers and mankind for a very long time. The earliest associations would probably have been to hunt the badger as a food item and for fat, hide and bristles. Over time badgers would have gained the respect of mankind for their cleanliness, strength and amazing determination. In this latter regard the word badger appears in the dictionary, and is defined amongst other things as, 'to pester or worry'. It is certainly true that when they have their mind set on a particular course, it can be very difficult indeed to persuade them into changing it.

In archaeological excavations badger bones have been found in midden heaps and grave diggings, and these finds probably mean that they were consumed as food by our ancestors. In one excavation a Celtic prince was discovered laid to rest on a bed of badger skins, leading one to assume that badger skins were once sought after for fine bedding or were of some ritual significance in the culture of the time. Even today one meets country people who remember eating badger hams, and using their fat as a cure for rheumatism.

From the penis of the badger comes a bone called the baculum. Conveniently it has a hole at each end and is the perfect length for a tie pin, and was once used in Scotland for this purpose. The skinned head of the badger was once used as the sporran decoration for the officers of the Argyll and Sutherland Highlanders.

The long stiff hairs from the badger's back were found to be perfect for shaving brushes, and though today most brushes are artificial, a visit to an art shop will turn up a genuine badger-bristle brush. However, it should be noted that these hairs must be imported from countries where the killing of badgers is still legal. The pelts themselves were sewn for rugs, and in some country districts, as waistcoats, before the widespread use of yarns. Amongst the records of big estates it is not uncommon

Badgers drink from a tree pool.

to find badgers on the list of animals that were hunted and killed. Indeed badgers were of such value as a quarry that they were reintroduced onto estates from which they had disappeared, for the sole purpose of the hunt.

The name of the badger, and its many derivations, occurs in people's names and place names across the entire country – Brocketsbrae, Broxburn, Brocklehurst, Brocksbank and many more. As an emblem the badger has even found its way into the boardroom of the supermarket chain Tesco, who have incorporated it into their coat of arms.

Conservation

For hundreds and hundreds of years it has been open season with regard to killing badgers. I still speak to older people today for whom a Sunday afternoon in their youth not spent killing badgers, as they saw it as a service to the countryside, would have been an afternoon all the poorer for it. The following conversation was with an elderly man from Cornwall: 'There was nothing wrong with it', he said, 'some folk played cricket, others went down to the pub, and we went down to the woods to dig out some badgers. We would knock them on the head with a spade and once they began to bleed from their nose they would surely die!' The details I have heard, along with the misconceptions about what people once thought (that badgers have longer legs on one side than the other so they run across slopes more easily), could fill the pages of this book.

Stories like these do however give a tiny glimpse of a time when myth and misunderstanding took the place of today's reason and scientific observation. There is no doubt that it is something of both perspectives that makes badgers so fascinating. Almost uniquely, badgers attract the public's attention. No other animal has groups all across the country solely dedicated to its conservation. Acting for all these groups is the National Federation of Badger Groups, aided in Scotland by the Scottish Badger Committee. Conferences and training courses are organised, where enthusiasts learn more and hence take the message out to a wider public and to

*Always on the alert, badgers regularly check for danger
by testing the air with their sensitive nose.*

local and national government. National campaigns are run on topics such as snaring and persecution, and Parliament is lobbied for changes in legislation. Success came about in recent years in the form of *The Protection of Badgers Act 1992*, which brought protection both for the animal and its sett, and has gone a long way to help in the badger's recovery, making them an increasingly familiar sight in the countryside.

County badger groups work at local level to further the cause of badger conservation. These groups, along with many committed individuals, are carrying out important work. Perhaps the most crucial task is surveying, which establishes population levels and location. This information can be used both to protect individual setts and clans, and to encourage the inclusion of badgers in local authority planning. Development (roads, housing, retail etc) has an effect on badgers, their territories and their food sources, and advice on badgers and their needs is something which badger workers are keen to ensure that planning departments, developers and the general public receive.

There is little doubt that the loss of areas of the countryside has a damaging effect on its wildlife as habitat is lost and populations become fragmented. There are many families of badgers who have become isolated from the countryside as housing, roads, and industrial developments encircle them, and their future can be extremely bleak. In some areas of the country so much of the

Warning! Badgers crossing.

Signs like these are increasingly used to help prevent road deaths.

badgers' natural foraging area has been removed that they are now dependent on handouts from local residents for their survival.

When tunnels collapse they can form new entrances.

Another major threat comes on the country's roads, where tens of thousands of badgers are killed each year. Here too it is possible to help badgers. Fencing can be installed along new roads to keep the badgers from crossing and, in conjunction with underpasses at places where they already cross, can provide an effective solution to the problem.

However, on some long-established roads badgers are regularly killed at their traditional crossing places. Sometimes it is not possible to install a tunnel under an existing road and in these cases signs can be erected to alert motorists and roadside reflectors to alert badgers.

Forestry also brings its problems for badgers when setts are threatened by felling and associated forestry operations. Careful felling can avoid crushing tunnels, and the retention of high tree stumps around the sett can prevent machinery crossing the area.

Unfortunately, the illegal 'sport' of badger baiting still goes on across the land. Men and dogs go to the woods and dig the badgers from their sett. The badger is then killed, or set upon by the dogs. This activity is made all the more barbaric when the badgers are taken away alive to be baited in pits against dogs in organised fights. Spectators can witness cruelty and death and bet on the outcome. In the long fight against this activity, badger groups and the conservation movement in general are calling increasingly on the police. Specially trained Wildlife Liaison Officers are now a common resource and are able to deal more effectively with wildlife crime.

Tuberculosis (TB), along with badger baiting, raises some of the most frequently asked questions of badger workers. The problem with TB is that the disease can affect cattle, badgers and man. For farmers in particular it can be devastating, as all the cattle on the farm have to be destroyed if an outbreak occurs. Despite decades of research and considerable government finance, there is still no credible solution in sight, and no proven link between TB in badgers and in cattle out in the fields. In the latest review, the lack of a clear solution has been recognised, and a radical policy has been proposed which involves three large areas of the country affected by TB.

In one area, all the badgers will be killed and any badgers entering the area will be trapped and shot. In the second area, the present policy of trapping and killing badgers only when there is an outbreak will be maintained, and in the third, a control area, there will be no killing of badgers even if there is an outbreak. Inevitably there is a great deal of debate as to the effectiveness of this plan and it still remains unclear if it will provide a solution. In the short term however, both the cost and the numbers of badgers killed continue to rise.

In the UK the level of interest in and protection of badgers is the highest in Europe. In other countries, even where the population is fragile, the number of activists is far fewer. In the Netherlands, where badger numbers are low, there are just a small number of activists fighting hard against the pressures of development. In Swedish forests the policy of badger protection is beginning to follow that started in Britain, and gradually other countries are being influenced. All this is due to the tireless hard work of a relative few.

Tracks, trails and signs, badgers leave them as clear evidence of their passing: from a five-toed footprint on a well trodden path, to hairs caught on a wire fence.

Getting Involved

Watching and studying badgers can be enormously rewarding, sitting in a quiet wood at dusk listening to the animals of the day settling down, followed by the animals of the night beginning to stir. An owl hoot here, a woodcock call there, then a bat flits past and a roe deer picks its way through the woods. The wind in the trees and the changing atmosphere as day gives way to night, the scents in the damp wood – all this and badgers too!

To watch badgers in relative comfort, choose a night between Easter and mid-August when the wind is from the south. The best time to watch cubs is in May when they first emerge, or June for boisterous play. Choose a badger sett well in advance of your watch on a steep south-facing slope with not too much cover. You do not need to hide because badgers cannot see you easily, although they will notice you if you move. Pick a seat about 100 ft (30.5 m) away, this will ensure that your scent will be blown away from the badgers most of the time. The view from your seat should be uninterrupted or you will be tempted to move about when you hear but can't see the badgers, and this may disturb them. Wear quiet clothes – the tearing of velcro and the jangling of buckles on wellies does no good. Take binoculars if you have them for good close-up views. Do not eat or drink. Keep still and wait.

Use cameras only when the badgers have become habituated to your watching. The actual flash does not normally affect the badger. However, a noisy flash mechanism and camera auto rewind will send them scurrying for cover.

We still have much to learn and there is a great deal that individuals can continue to contribute to our understanding. If you would like to find out more and perhaps get involved then contact the National Federation of Badger Groups or your local Wildlife Trust for your nearest group. Some useful names and addresses are listed at the back of this book.

This favourite British animal is still under threat from persecution and development.

*With their fluffed-up tails badger cubs are very inquisitive, eager
to discover their mysterious world guided by the adults.*

Badgers of the World

Across the world on four continents there are a total of six different badgers belonging to the subfamily Melinae. Added to this is the Honey Badger of the subfamily Mellivorinae which, although not a true badger, shares many features in common with Melinae.

Eurasian Badger (*Meles meles*)

A familiar representative of the countryside throughout the UK. The Eurasian badger is a medium-sized carnivore, with a wide distribution, from Eire in the west, to Japan in the east. It occurs in many countries in between, including Russia, Iran, China and all the European countries. Across this vast area the badger's lifestyle changes to meet the demands of mountains, arid landscapes, harsh winters and man-made environments.

Honey Badger (*Mellivora capensis*)

This animal occurs in sub-Saharan Africa and through the Middle East as far as India. Although the same size as the Eurasian Badger they have a fearsome reputation, having been recorded killing buffalo by attacking them in the scrotum and also being observed seeing lions off a kill.

Chinese Ferret Badgers

(*Melogale mosquata, M. personata & M. everetti*)
There are three known species of this small primitive genus occurring through China, Borneo and Java. These badgers live mainly in tropical and sub-tropical forests, feeding on small animals, invertebrates and wild fruit.

Indonesian Stink Badger (*Mydaus javensis*) and Palawan Stink Badger (*Suillotaxus marchei*)

Both live in the forests of the Indonesian Islands. Their common name derives from their ability to squirt anal gland secretions at aggressors. Little is known about their diet or general habits, but they have been eaten as food in the past and their secretions have been used as a constituent of perfume.

Hog Badgers (*Arctonyx collaris*)

Hog badgers live in south-east Asia and in China. Their distribution overlaps with the Eurasian badger, which they resemble both in size and general characteristics. The hog badger also forages rather than hunts for its food, and is omnivorous.

American Badgers (*Taxidea taxus*)

American badgers have a similar appearance to the Eurasian, the chief difference being a lack of the characteristic stripe which is replaced by a thin white line from the nose over its head between the ears. It is primarily a hunter, feeding on small mammals which it catches by digging them out of their burrows.

*For 60,000 millenia, badgers have stalked the woods and fields of the
world, alongside the bats and owls, wolves and beavers. As we retire
to our beds, rest assured the badgers are out there, still foraging.*

Badger Facts

Badger	From the French word *becheur* meaning digger
Male	Boar
Female	Sow
Young	Cub
Sett	From the ancient word *cete* meaning a group of badgers
Other	brock, pate, grey, badget (Old English)
names	brocklach (Scottish Gaelic)
	broc (Irish Gaelic)
Weight	Males 22 lbs (10 kgs)
	Females 20 lbs (9 kgs)
	Weights vary seasonally and can be 55 lbs (25 kgs) or more
Length	Males 36 in (903 mm)
	Females 34 in (874 mm)
Vocalisation	Wickering, yelps and low growls
Breeding	Peak time February
Gestation	After delayed implantation, 6 or 7 weeks
Birth	Peak time February
Litter size	1–5
	Average 2–3
Cubs emerge	Late April / May
Legislation	*The Protection of Badgers Act 1992* gives legal protection to badgers and their setts. It is an offence to cruelly ill-treat a badger or disturb one in its sett.

Recommended Reading

Clark, M., *Badgers*, Whittet, 1994.

Cox, P., *Badgers on Site. A Guide for Developers and Planners*, Berks County Council, 1993.

Forestry Authority, The, *Forest Operations and Badger Setts*, The Forestry Commission, 1995.

Krukk, H., *The Social Badger*, Oxford University Press, 1989.

Neal, E.G. & Cheeseman C., *Badgers*, Poyser Natural History, 1996.

RSPCA, *Problems With Badgers*, RSPCA, Causeway, Horsham, West Sussex, 1984.

Contacts

Countryside Council For Wales
Plas Penrhos
Ffordd Penrhos
Bangor
Gwynedd
LL57 2LQ
Tel: 01248 370444

English Nature
Northminster House
Northminster Road
Cambridge PE1 1UA
Tel: 01733 455000

The National Federation
of Badger Groups
Conservation Officer
2 Cloisters Business Centre
8 Battersea Park Road,
London
SW8 4BG
Tel: 0171 498 3220

RSPCA
Causeway, Horsham
West Sussex RH12 1HG
Tel: 0140 326 4181

Scottish Natural Heritage
2 Anderson Place
Edinburgh EH6 5NP
Tel: 0131 554 9797

The Scottish Wildlife Trust
Cramond House
Kirk Cramond
Cramond Glebe Road
Edinburgh EH4 6NS
Tel: 0131 312 7765

The Wildlife Trusts
The Green, Witham Park
Waterside South
Lincoln LN5 7JR
Tel: 01522 544400

Biographical Note

LAURIE CAMPBELL developed an interest in natural history from an early age and has been photographing wildlife for some 25 years. His work features in books, magazines and television programmes around the world. He is a four-time award winner in the BBC Wildlife Photographer of the Year competition and author of two previous books: *The Wildlife Photographs of Laurie Campbell* and the *RSPB Guide to Nature Photography*.

JOHN DARBYSHIRE, has held a lifelong interest in the natural environment and wrote his first paper on badgers, age 20. Now a ranger for the Scottish Wildlife Trust in the Clyde Valley, he established and runs Scotland's premier badger watch programme. Also a professional wildlife consultant and founder of the Lanarkshire Badger Group, he advises at a national level through the Scottish Badger Committee.